RUCKSACK GUIDE
Alpinism

ALUN RICHARDSON

ILLUSTRATED BY GEORGE MANLEY

A&C BLACK • LONDON

Published by A & C Black Publishers Ltd
36 Soho Square, London W1D 3QY
www.acblack.com

ISBN 978 0 7136 8685 2

A CIP catalogue record for this book is available from the British Library.

Acknowledgements
Cover photograph © Alun Richardson
Inside photographs © Alun Richardson except p.6 Kristjan Maack and
   p.8 Shaun Hutson
Illustrations by © George Manley, except p. 51 © Crown Copyright
   (2008), the Met Office
Designed by James Watson
Commisioned by Robert Foss
Edited by Lucy Beevor

This book is produced using paper that is made from wood grown in
managed, sustainable forests. It is natural, renewable and recyclable.
The logging and manufacturing processes conform to the environmental
regulations of the country of origin.

Typeset in 9pt on 10pt Din-Light by Margaret Brain, UK

Printed and bound in China by C&C Offset Printing Co., Ltd.

ACKNOWLEDGEMENTS

The ideas in this book are the culmination of 25 years mountaineering and time spent discussing techniques with inspirational climbers, Mountain Guides and instructors, in particular Alan Dance, Dave Williams, Steve Lewis, Graeme Ettle, Bruce Goodlad, Eric PirieTrevor Massiah, Jim Beynon, Clive Hebblethwaite, John Taylor, Twid Turner, Louise Thomas and Pat Littlejohn.

Special thanks to Lesley Jones who supported me throughout; Clive Hebblethwaite who supplied some of the photographs; Dr Jim Duff for his advice on acclimatisation; Rhiannon Richardson and Molly Jones for help with text and diagrams; George Manley for his excellent illustrations; Robert Foss and Lucy Beevor from A&C Black; and the manufacturers who generously supported the photo shoots: DMM, Lyon Equipment, Mountain Equipment, Face West, Select Solar, Mammut and Fritschi.

Any of the opinions expressed in this book are mine alone and should not be associated with any of the above people, companies or organisations.

Alpinism is the sixth book in the **Rucksack Guide** series and covers the skills required to become a competent alpine mountaineer. This handy book can be kept in your rucksack and will help you to gain the experience to mountaineer safely anywhere in the world. Many of the skills required for competent alpinism are the same as traditional rock climbing and winter mountaineering. This book does not cover the technical aspects of navigation, rock, snow and ice climbing (see **Rucksack Guides** to *Mountain Walking and Trekking*, *Rock Climbing* and *Winter Mountaineering* for further information).

The **Rucksack Guide** series tells you *what* to do in a situation, but it does not always explain *why*. If you want more information behind the decisions in these books, go to *Mountaineering: The Essential Skills for Mountaineers and Climbers* by Alun Richardson (A&C Black, 2008).

For more information about the author, his photographs and the courses he runs go to:

www.freedomphotographs.co.uk or
www.alunrichardson.org.

Alpinism is not controlled adventure like sport climbing or climbing on a roadside crag; it is real adventure, in which you have to rely more on your awareness and judgement than your technical skills. Luckily there are challenges to suit everyone's ambitions, experience and abilities, including glacial walking, non-technical and technical routes on low- or high-altitude mountains.

A non-technical peak can be described as one where one axe will suffice, yet the ascent requires fitness and an understanding of objective dangers such as altitude, rock fall and avalanche. General crampon, ice axe and rope work skills are required for crossing glaciers and ascending easier snow slopes. A technical peak usually involves all of the above, as well as scrambling, rock-climbing and/or ice climbing techniques.

Alpinism refers to mountaineering in areas such as the Rocky Mountains, the Cascades and the Sierra Nevada in the United States, and the Canadian Rockies. For UK climbers, the European Alps are a useful stepping-stone to expedition climbing, because the mountains are more remote, logistics are difficult and rescue is largely down to the climbers themselves.

Many of the skills required for competent alpinism are the same as traditional rock climbing and winter mountaineering or climbing. They are applied here to the European Alps, but the principles also apply to alpine mountain ranges around the world.

Fig.1 Climbers on Peigne d'Arolla, Swiss Alps

Climbing quickly is the essence of safe alpinism, as you are exposed to the danger zone for less time, and it enables you to reach the summit and descend before the afternoon storms catch you. Being fit and a good climber are obvious assets, but efficiency is synonymous with climbing light – if you carry everything you are probably going to need it!

Unlike Scotland in winter, you will experience extremes of temperature in the same day, meaning a flexible clothing system is essential. Invest in a good pair of Schoeller-type mountaineering trousers and always carry a warm hat and gloves. Consider shorts and a T-shirt for the walk to the hut. Wear combinations of layers and ventilate/remove the layers to stay dry.

- **Next to the skin** Use a performance wicking fabric, such as polypropylene, that wicks perspiration away from your skin to the mid-layer. Avoid cotton.
- **Mid-layer** Use a thicker synthetic fleece to hold in the heat.
- **Insulating layer** A thicker fleece or a soft shell jacket is ideal for the summer. A light down jacket is a good idea for high mountain trips.
- **Waterproof layer** Most of the time the weather will be good, so use lightweight waterproof shells for emergency protection.

EXPERT TIP

Richard Mansfield
IFMGA Mountain Guide
www.mountain-guides.net

'Climbing lightweight: light, plus light, plus light equals heavy.'

Fig. 2 You can save weight on nearly every piece of kit, from krabs to your rucksack. (Climbers on Monch Bernese Oberland, Switzerland.)

Boots suitable for alpine use will have room for your toes to wriggle, be stiffer and have a sharp edge to the sole for kicking into snow slopes. You can wear a pair of running shoes for the hut walk (leave them at the hut if you are coming back the same way).

BOOT TYPES		
Type	Pro	Con
Leather boots	● Good for climbing mixed routes in less-than Arctic conditions ● Provide a more precise feel	● Not as warm ● Less waterproof
Plastic boots	● Provide warmth ● Provide good support for ice climbing ● Waterproof	● Mostly heavier ● Less sensitive ● The shells cover two size ranges, with a thicker inner to pad out the smaller size. This collapses over time.

To make the issue of boot/crampon compatibility more straightforward, boots and crampons can be graded according to their basic design and intended use. However, not all manufacturers follow the system designed by Scarpa (Fig. 6, p.11).

BOOT COMPATIBILITY

Graded B0 to B3, dependent on the stiffness of the sole and the support provided by the uppers:

- **B0** Flexible walking boots. Any boot that can be bent more than half an inch when standing on the front edge will be less suitable for use with all crampon types.

- **B1** Stiff mountain walking boots suitable only for use with C1 crampons (p.10).

- **B2** Very stiff mountaineering boots suitable only for use with C1 or C2 crampons.

- **B3** Fully rigid, winter climbing and mountaineering boots suitable for use with C1, C2 or C3 crampons.

Fig. 3 *A sturdy pair of boots with room for your toes to wriggle is essential for warmth and stability on snow.*

LOOKING AFTER YOUR FEET

Feet have little muscle bulk and it is much easier to keep them warm than to warm them up.

- On long belays, avoid standing on snow, weight your feet equally and stamp your feet when they start to chill.
- Try to minimise the body closing down the extremities by dressing according to the route and climate, and don't scrimp on leg protection.
- Keep your feet dry, even if it means changing your socks during the day.
- Wear gaiters (p.15).
- Foot powder with aluminium hydroxide can help to reduce perspiration.

For information on vapour barrier liners see *Rucksack Guide: Mountaineering in Remote Areas of the World* (A&C Black, 2009).

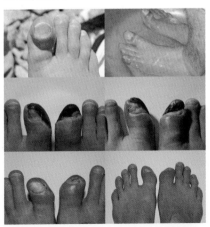

Fig. 4 *The development of frostbite at 30 hours; 4 days; 35 days; 75 days; 178 days (post-op); and 250 days.*

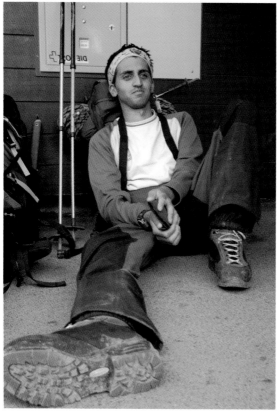

Fig. 5 *Alpine boots must be able to cope with walking to huts and climbing on technical rock , snow and ice.*

Crampons and boots make an integral unit – using the wrong type of crampon on the wrong type of boot can break them or cause them to fall off the boot.

Crampons are graded C1 to C3, depending on their attachment method and flexibility. When buying crampons, always take your boots with you and fit the crampons in the store.

CRAMPON COMPATIBILITY

- **C1** Lightweight articulated or flexible walking crampons with simple straps. Most commonly 10 point (2 front and 8 bottom). They are light, simple and a good choice for occasional use (low-angle snow, glacier crossing).

- **C2** Articulated or flexible step-in crampons attached with a heel clip and toe strap. Most commonly 12 point (4 front and 8 bottom). They give the best balance between ease of attachment, walking comfort and climbing performance. A good choice for general mountaineering and low- to mid-grade ice climbs.

- **C3** Stiffer, or even fully rigid, crampons attached with a heel clip and toe bail. They usually have 12 or more points, and adjustable front points (mono or dual). They are the best choice for pure ice and climbing performance, but a pain for general alpine mountaineering/walking.

TERRAIN	CRAMPON			BOOT		
Low-level walking	C1	C2		B1	B2	B3
Mountaineering						
Snow routes Grades 1–2						
Snow routes Grade 3 up			C3			
Buttress climbing						
Mixed climbing and ice-fall climbing						

Fig. 6 Crampon/boot compatibility table

Fig. 7 A good general mountaineering crampon will do a better job on waterfall ice than a waterfall ice crampon will do in the mountains.

TIPS FOR FITTING AND USING CRAMPONS

- The sole of your boot should match the shape of the crampon, without any large gaps.
- A correctly adjusted crampon should remain attached to the boot with the straps and clips undone.
- Put crampons in a crampon bag and carry them inside your pack.
- Trim the straps to a sensible length (long, dangling straps can catch on the other crampon), but allow enough length to put over the top of your gaiters.
- Check all boots and screws are tight, that straps are not cut or damaged, and that there are no cracks in the linking bar or crampon.
- If you forget anti-balling plates, use a plastic bag and tape, but do not expect it to last for very long.
- Carry plastic ties, a strap, some cord and a small nut and bolt to repair crampons.

FRONT POINTS

- Front points should stick out by 25–35mm.
- Front points that are drooped and the second row angled forward are more suited to ice climbing. The angled second points reduce calf strain by resting against the ice.
- Downward-facing second points facilitate a more ergonomic walking motion.
- Horizontally orientated front points are more versatile and perform better than vertically orientated ones for pure ice climbing.

- Vertical front points also tend to come out of the ice more easily when the heel is raised. However, vertical mono points do provide more precision and are the best choice for very steep, hard ice and mixed ground. If the route is predominantly firm snow or ice, stick with two.

SHARPENING CRAMPON POINTS

- Sharpen the points with a hand file, not a grinder – the heat generated makes the points brittle.
- For moderate mountaineering, sharpen front points once a season and leave the rest of the points as they are.
- For harder routes, the sharpness and length of your front and secondary points is more important.
- A modular design crampon allows you to replace just the front points.
- Vertical technical points need not be razor sharp like a pick, but should have a point so that you can stand on the smallest edges.

CRAMPONS

When buying crampons always take your boots with you and fit the crampons in store. They are all slightly different – some suit narrower boots, some suit boots with a thicker sole, some will not fit boots with too much of a 'rocker' (curved section of the sole). For those of you with narrow feet, avoid crampons that have a wide spread between the front points and check the length of the points ... they may well be too long.

CLIMBING LIGHT

CRAMPON ATTACHMENTS
There are three attachment systems:

1. **Strap on** Useful in exceptional circumstances, e.g. for high altitude boots, but they have been superceded by a plastic heel cup and plastic front bail found on most C1 crampons. They will fit on boots without a heel and toe clip.

2. **Step-in** A wire toe bail fits over the welt and a heel tension lever snaps into place on the heel. The system typically includes an ankle strap. It's a secure system for plastic boots and leather boots with plastic soles that have deep notches on toes and heels. Correctly fitted, these are fast, vibration-free and easy to use but, for most climbers, a mixed binding is better, because they are easier to put on when your boots are iced up and safer as the boot welt wears down.

3. **Mixed simple** Efficient and suitable for most uses, except steep waterfall ice climbs. The heel attaches with a lever and the toes attach with a strap and a ring or a plastic bail. These bindings can be used with lighter mountaineering boots, without heavy welts.

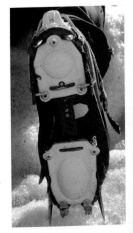

Fig. 8 Anti-balling plates are essential to prevent the build-up of snow on the underside of crampons, especially in wet snow conditions (the traditional remedy is to tap your crampons with your ice axe, but this is awkward, time consuming and distracting).

A good quality gaiter should be waterproof. Nylon is cheap, but not breathable, and canvas is durable, but stiff. Gore Tex is breathable, but expensive and doesn't breath when dirty. Elastic or lace bindings under the boot are easy to use, but rubberised or cable straps last longer. Velcro closures are easier to use and keep water out, but a zippered closure with a good storm flap will work better.

Gaiters come in three designs:

1 **Low (stop tous)** Ankle-high and cooler, less able to keep rain and snow out, but my choice for most conditions.

2 **High** Calf-high and helpful when you are walking in deep snow on wet, muddy trails, wading through streams, or crashing through vegetation.

3 **Full, over-the-boot** Useful when doing a lot of walking in deep snow or very wet, boggy terrain, because they turn the boot into a Wellington. But they can be too warm, are expensive, and the rubber erodes easily, particularly the instep.

Fig. 9 Love them or hate them, gaiters keep the snow out of your boots!

- Get the simplest and lightest 30–50 litre sac that will carry your load comfortably. You may sacrifice durability, but you will enjoy your trip much more.
- Choose a narrow profile with compression straps, an extendable lid, a lightweight hip belt, and cut off anything that is not necessary.
- Lightweight sacs rarely have a back adjustment system, so you must purchase the correct size and pack it carefully.
- Place heavy items next to your back.
- A rucksack is not waterproof so store gear in watertight bags.
- For balance, pack your rucksack to keep heavy items below your shoulders, close to your back and centred between your shoulder blades.
- Make sure you can look up without your helmet hitting the sac.

A CORRECTLY ADJUSTED RUCKSACK
On a correctly adjusted or sized rucksack:

- The shoulder strap will curve neatly over the shoulder when the hip belt is sitting correctly (Fig. 10).
- The top of your hip should sit in the middle of the padded belt to transfer the load to the top of the buttocks.
- Tensioning straps link the top of the rucksack to the top of the shoulder straps and pull the rucksack closer to your back to improve stability. They can be released when going downhill to keep the rucksack upright.
- Carry walking poles, tent poles, sleeping mats etc down the compression straps.

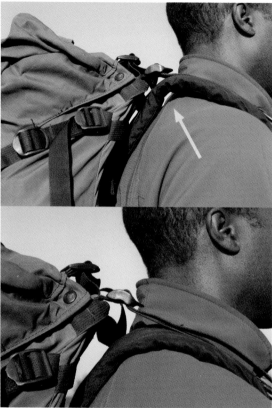

Fig. 10 *On a correctly adjusted or sized rucksack the shoulder strap will curve neatly over the shoulder (bottom).*

HELMETS

Stonefall is a real problem in the Alps. The impact of even a small stone is enough to cause serious injury, so wear the best, but lightest, helmet (however, beware that rocks can hit you anywhere on the body). Comfort is the most important factor – if it's not comfortable, you won't wear it.

There are two types of helmet:

1 **Hard shell models** Constructed from plastic, fibreglass or carbon fibre composites. Hard shells are the 'classic' mountaineering helmets with a hard shell outer and an inner cradle.

2 **Injected foam models** Much lighter (up to 50 per cent), but less durable. In general, the new lightweight foam helmets absorb less energy during an impact from above than more 'traditional' designs. Where stonefall is common, or when ice climbing, a hard shell is probably better, but a lightweight model means that you will wear it all day.

Fitting

The helmet should not flop over your eyes or expose the front of the skull when you look up. Ensure it fits over a warm hat, will accept a head torch, and that you can still look upwards while wearing a rucksack.

SUNGLASSES

UV radiation in the high mountains is extreme. Wear a wide brimmed hat and glasses with category four lenses and full-wrap sides to stop light leaking in. Avoid side shields that can impair your vision. Carry a spare pair between two climbers. Clip-on sunglasses are not adequate; if you wear glasses get prescription sunglasses, or wear disposable contact lenses. Goggles are generally unnecessary in summer, but they can always act as a spare pair of sunglasses.

GLASSES AND CONTACT LENSES

Contact lenses can be used successfully, but as everyone is constrained to wear sunglasses once above the snowline, it is easier to wear sunglasses with prescription lenses. Opticians regularly make them, but it is not always easy to get a pair suitable for mountaineering, i.e. those that have been designed to ensure little light enters from the sides, bottom or around the nose. Close-fitting, wrap-around style glasses are common, but these don't always come with the option of taking prescription lenses. The easiest and most cost-effective solution is to buy standard mountaineering sunglasses from an outdoor shop and then to have them re-glazed by an optician with prescription lenses, darkened with your preferred tint, and other lens coatings such as extra UV filters.

Fig. 11 Snow reflects 85 per cent of UV and the intensity increases by 10 per cent every 1000m.

SUNSCREEN AND LIP BLOCK

Skin cancer is the most common form of cancer, yet protecting the body is simple. Use sunscreen with a minimum SPF of 15 (more is better). Zinc oxide or titanium dioxide blocks out all of the Sun's rays, and both are especially good for the nose, lips (which are particularly vulnerable, because they lack melatonin), and for people with fair skin. However, sunscreen alone does not offer enough protection, so be sure to wear protective clothing.

HEAD TORCH

Hand-held torches are useless because you often require the use of both hands. Head torches with LEDs are small, lightweight and powerful. They produce a brighter and clearer high-quality light than standard bulbs, operate in all temperatures and are virtually unbreakable. Choose a lightweight LED model.

MOUNTAINEERING ICE AXE

For non-technical routes a lightweight T-rated single general mountaineering axe is enough. Ensure that the handle's diameter is small enough for you to hold with gloves on. What length the ideal axe should be is controversial, but the answer is simple: the steeper the slope, the more experienced you are, and the more proficient on crampons you are, the shorter the axe can be.

- Models with a gently curved shaft have a better swing and do not compromise the ability to plunge them into the snow. However, on easier angled slopes (less than 60 degrees) they have no real advantage over straight models.

- A hand rest makes it easier to grip the shaft and prevents you from banging your knuckles against the ice. The hand rest does not appreciably affect plunging the axe into the snow.

- A rubber grip on the shaft keeps your hands warmer, dampens any vibration and helps you to grip the axe. However, it can hinder you plunging the axe into hard snow.

- Ultra-light models without a spike can become blocked and do not perform well in harder snow and ice.

Ratings and standards

There are two CE marks (European standard – see www.uiaa.ch/?c=310 for details) for ice axes:

- **B-rated (Basic) axes** Intended for hill walking and glacier walking. They have shafts strong enough to use as a belay anchor.

- **T-rated (Technical) tools** Intended for climbing and mountaineering. They are 30–40 per cent stronger to allow for more extreme use and abuse, such as torquing the picks into cracks.

Picks also have B and T ratings. T-rated picks are thicker to withstand the side-to-side stress test. However, they are not as good for penetrating ice. Whichever you use, it is very difficult to break an ice pick. For information on technical ice axes see *Rucksack Guide: Winter Mountaineering*.

Fig. 12 *Tape thin closed-cell foam over the top of your ice axe to protect your hands from the cold.*

HARNESS

Get the lightest available, ensuring it fits over all of your layers and is secure when wearing the base layer alone. When rock climbing you require a fully specified harness (four gear loops etc), whereas you only need a minimum of features on your harness when you are non-technical mountaineering.

To make it easier to go to the toilet, adapt the harness by dropping the leg loops from the rear. Gear loops that hang from the bottom of the waist belt extend below your rucksack, giving you easier access to your gear.

Fig. 13 *A DMM alpine harness is simple and lightweight, and can be easily put on when wearing crampons.*

HARDWEAR

Success on an alpine peak usually involves climbing lots of moderate- to medium-difficulty ground fast. The hardest thing, therefore, is making your rack light enough to move quickly, yet large enough to be safe (researching your route should help you to decide what to take).

ROPES

- Use a 9.5–9.7mm single rope on less technical routes to save weight.
- If you know the route well, you can carry very specific lengths, in some cases as little as 30m of 9mm for non-technical climbs.
- Two dry-coated 60m 9mm double ropes are best for technical climbs.
- With so many sharp edges around avoid super-thin half ropes.
- 50m ropes are lighter, but the extra 10m of a 60m rope reduces the number of stances.

EMERGENCY KIT

Take the following:

- A two-person group shelter or a plastic survival bag. Foil blankets are a waste of time as they flap around and do not keep out the elements.
- A small foam pad to sit on.
- A small stove, pan, windshield and some instant soups. The Jet Boil and MSR Reactor stoves do not require separate pans and work well in the wind.

HANDS

- Keep your core temperature up and your hands dry (don't put wet hands into gloves).
- Your wrist has the third-highest heat loss of the body, so make sure the sleeves on your layers are long enough and carry fleece wrist-overs.
- Carry a waterproof shell glove or mitt and several pairs of thin and thick fleece gloves with sticky palms. Change them whenever they are wet and your hands cold.
- Avoid gloves with a floating liner because they are difficult to get on and off, and carry a pair of fleece mitts that are easily accessible at belays and for when it is really cold.
- Attach all gloves to your wrist by a keeper cord.

HEAD

- Wear a fleece hat or balaclava under your helmet.
- A fleece neck gaiter or a fleece jacket with a hood will seal your neck and prevent heat loss during long belays.

EXPERT TIP

Shaun Hutson
shaun@sphutson.com

'Just because you have had very cold feet and hands in oxygen-rich lower altitudes without frostbite, don't think you can apply the same approach to higher altitudes. Frostbite is often the result of ignoring a bit of the body.'

Staying warm not only depends on clothing, but also on your water and energy levels.

- Eat a good breakfast and keep your energy levels up by eating small amounts of food (e.g. grain bars, dried fruit, bananas, peanut butter sandwiches) every 30 minutes or so.
- Smoking reduces peripheral circulation and can increase the chances of cold extremities.
- A 5 per cent drop in hydration levels can reduce performance by up to 50 per cent.
- Drink plenty two hours before going out, and a lot when you return. Water intake in hot environments should be about 2l a day.
- Hydration bladders are great, but are expensive, freeze in the cold and can tempt you to finish all your water too quickly.
- A warm drink is only psychologically different to a cold one (the energy content keeps you warm, not the heat).

EARLY SIGNS OF DEHYDRATION

- Headache
- Light-headedness
- Lethargy
- A vague feeling of being unwell.

DRINKING WATER FROM STREAMS AND RIVERS

Advice is varied, and it depends on the source of the water. It is probably safe to drink stream water high up in the mountains where there are no animals grazing. Avoid alpine stream water from glaciers, because the tiny mineral particles can upset your digestive system. Inside Science News Service reported that water from springs, wells and long-term ground water is usually pure and wholesome. The Mountaineering Council of Scotland states that mountain streams in the UK well away from human habitation can be drunk untreated, but avoid oil-covered peat sources. Treat water if in doubt.

Fig. 14 Is it safe to drink water from an alpine stream?

ENERGY AND REHYDRATION DRINKS

Two main factors affect the absorption of fluid into the body:

1   The speed at which it empties from the stomach. This depends on the carbohydrate content – the higher it is, the slower your stomach empties.

2 The rate at which it is absorbed through the walls of the small intestine.

'Energy' drinks and fruit juices are not suitable for rehydration, because they slow down stomach emptying and may even draw fluids into the stomach and away from the body. Artificial sweeteners also cause dehydration, because they draw fluid from the large intestine.

Conversely, salts – especially sodium and potassium – in a drink allow fluid to empty quickly from the stomach and promote absorption from the small intestine, thereby encouraging hydration. Isotonic sports drinks (in balance with the body's salts) or – even better – hypotonic sports drinks (lower than the body's salts) with a carbohydrate level of approximately 6 per cent are emptied from the stomach at a rate similar to water and may be beneficial if you are walking for hours and cannot eat. However, save the extra plastic bottle – a banana and plain water will probably work just as well.

Check the additives in sports drinks, because some are dangerous for mountaineering. For example, norepinephrine is a vasoconstrictor (narrows the blood vessels), which can be dangerous in cold climates.

MAKE YOUR OWN REHYDRATION DRINK

It is easy to make 1l of rehydration drink at a fraction of the price, also avoiding using plastic bottles:

- Isotonic – 500ml of unsweetened fruit juice and 500ml of water
- Hypotonic – 100ml of squash, 900ml of water and a pinch of salt.

Alpinism takes place in mountain ranges where access is not too problematic, but the approaches involve crossing glaciers. The routes can be long and success requires a high level of commitment, judgement and fitness. With altitude problems, stone fall and violent electrical storms, this is an environment with many potential hazards. You can reduce the risks by understanding what they are and when they might occur.

BERGSHRUND

A bergschrund is a crevasse that marks the point where a glacier meets the snow on a mountain. They extend to the bedrock and can be very deep, filling with snow and presenting a difficult obstacle to the alpiniste.

Fig. 15 *The features of an Alpine peak*

1 Gendarmes	15 Glacier
2 Horn or aiguilles	16 Truncated spur
3 Cornice	17 Avalanche debris
4 Ridge	18 Hanging glacier
5 Couloir or gully	19 Crevasses
6 Rognon	20 Medial moraine
7 Rock arête	21 Lateral moraine
8 Bergschrund	22 Roche moutonnée
9 Cirque or bowl	23 Snout
10 Firn line	24 Moraine lake
11 Sercas	25 Outwash plain
12 Ice fall	26 Terminal moraine
13 Nunatak	27 Erratic boulder
14 Snow field	

(With thanks to Dr J. Duff). As you go higher, the percentage of oxygen remains the same, but the pressure drops and the number of oxygen molecules per breath is reduced. The lower air pressure not only makes it more difficult for your lungs to absorb oxygen, but also affects your brain, digestive system and can cause fluid to leak into the lungs and the brain.

ALTITUDE		
Type	Height (m)	Height (ft)
High altitude	1500–3500	4921–11,483
Very high altitude	3500–5500	11,483–18,045
Extreme altitude	5500+	18,045+

ACCLIMATISATION

The good news is that, as you ascend progressively to higher altitude, your body's chemistry and physiology adapts to the lower oxygen levels.

Everybody can acclimatise; it is a matter of allowing enough time. If you ascend too quickly, you risk potentially lethal acute mountain sickness (AMS) or high altitude pulmonary oedema (HAPE) and high altitude cerebral oedema (HACE).

Virtually all climbers will experience some of the symptoms of AMS. If you have been slow to acclimatise on previous trips, the same pattern is likely on subsequent trips. Your chance of being affected is not dependent on age, gender or fitness.

To acclimatise:

- You must gently stress your body – too little and you will not adapt, too fast and you will become ill.
- The actual altitude is not important; it is how fast you ascend that matters. It is safer (and more enjoyable) to climb gradually and slowly — you can descend as fast as you like!
- Above 3000m you should make a slow and gradual ascent with an ideal height gain of 300m from the last place you slept to your next overnight stop. The sleeping altitude is particularly important — it is fine to go higher each day as long as you descend to sleep lower.
- Keeping to 300m is not always possible, but you should be aware of the potential problems if you make that jump too quickly.
- A rest day after every three days or after ascending to a point 1000m higher is recommended.

EXPERT TIP

Kenton Cool
www.dream-guides.com

'Acclimatising properly not only helps to prevent serious oedemas, but allows you to climb faster, better and efficiently, which is safer and more fun.'

THE ALPINE ENVIRONMENT

The symptoms of AMS are due to your body's failure to acclimatise. Symptoms usually start 12—24 hours after arrival at altitude and tend to worsen at night. HACE is considered to be the extreme end of the AMS spectrum. Mild AMS is not life threatening, but as it becomes more pronounced it will start to interfere with normal activity. You have acclimatised when the symptoms disappear and sleep becomes settled. Ascent to a higher altitude will require further acclimatisation, but on descent to lower altitude the beneficial effects only last for eight days.

There are no signs of mild AMS, only symptoms. A diagnosis is made when there is a headache plus one or more of the following: nausea, vomiting, loss of appetite, dizziness, fatigue or weakness, poor sleep (periodic breathing). Do not hide your symptoms, because you will not recognise when you are slipping into HACE or HAPE. If the patient is not improving, descend (600m) administer oxygen and give medication.

AMS SCORING

Symptom	Score
Headache	1
Nausea/loss of appetite	1
Insomnia	1
Giddiness	1
Headache after painkillers	2
Vomiting	2
Difficulty breathing at rest	3
Abnormal or intense fatigue	3
Decreased urination	3
Treatment	**Score**
Light AMS painkillers	1–3
Moderate AMS painkillers, rest and no ascent	4–6
Descend	>6

TREATMENT

AMS is treated with rest at the same altitude, rehydration, warmth, food and painkillers (Ibuprofen is best, although paracetamol is also safe). Giving 125–250mg Diamox (acetazolamide) every 12 hours and oxygen speeds up the process of acclimatisation. Painkillers and acetazolamide do not mask the symptoms of altitude illness.

The more serious altitude illnesses of High Altitude Pulmonary Oedema (HAPE) and High Altitude Cerebral Oedema (HACE) occur more frequently above 3500m, and are brought on by ascending too rapidly. HAPE is twice as common as HACE and is more likely to kill. They may occur together, so if you find one, check for the other. If you feel unwell at altitude, it is altitude illness until proven otherwise.

Fig. 16 *This is a trekker on Mt Kilimanjaro being dragged upwards, despite his AMS (he is one symptom short of near-death). The mountains will always be there – will you?*

HAPE is the leakage of fluid into and around the lungs, reducing your ability to absorb oxygen. Respiratory infections increase the risk and it is also antagonised by cold temperatures and exercise. AMS can precede HAPE, but it does occur alone.

POSSIBLE SYMPTOMS

- Loss of energy.
- More than usual breathlessness.
- A cough that starts off dry, becoming bubbly and wet with frothy sputum, which may be blood-stained.
- Rate of breathing (breaths per minute) and heart rate rise disproportionately at rest.
- May hear crackles in the lungs with a stethoscope once the disease is advanced.
- May be a mild fever, making it difficult to distinguish from pneumonia (infection of the lungs), which has sometimes led to fatal misdiagnosis.
- The lips and nail beds take on a bluish tinge (cyanosis), because fluid in the lungs prevents oxygen getting into the blood and unconsciousness occurs.

TREATMENT

- If available, give oxygen immediately, either from a bottle or by using a portable hyperbaric chamber (PHC), available in some alpine huts (remember that descent is the definitive treatment – do not delay once the patient has recovered sufficiently).
- Minimise exertion, which worsens HAPE – carry the patient (they may need to be sitting or propped up), assist them or at least carry their pack.
- Keep the patient warm and hydrated and give them food or a sugary drink.
- The drug nifedipine is used to prevent recurrence during descent.

Fig. 17 *Igor Gamow designed the first commercial PHC in the 1980s.*

HACE is the end-stage of AMS. It can develop very quickly. Death is due to the accumulation of fluid in and around the brain, which increases the pressure within the skull.

Whilst AMS and HACE may be linked, don't expect casualties to necessarily exhibit mild symptoms of AMS before presenting with clear symptoms of HACE (or HAPE). Depending on the rate of ascent and any one person's ability to acclimatise, symptoms of HACE and HAPE can present very quickly, for example in someone who only the evening before appeared quite well.

POSSIBLE SYMPTOMS

- Severe headache and vomiting, but absence of a headache must not be taken as absence of HACE. (If someone is hallucinating near the summit of Mt Kilimanjaro then, headache or not, they are one symptom short of near death).

- Lack of physical coordination (clumsy hands and unsteady feet) and, as the condition progresses, they may not be able to walk at all, and will stagger or fall when asked to stand upright (especially when they close their eyes).

- Mental symptoms – any or all of the following: confusion, disorientation, irrationality, unusual quietness or noisiness, hallucinations.

- Eventual sleepiness and lethargy before slipping into a coma and dying.

TREATMENT

- If available, give oxygen immediately either from a bottle or by using a portable hyperbaric chamber (but remember that descent is the definitive treatment – do not delay once the patient has recovered sufficiently).

- Administer dexamethasone regularly.

- Carry the patient or assist to descend.
- Clumsiness can persist for days, even weeks, despite the patient's apparent recovery.

ABOVE 7000M

Even when fully acclimatised, avoid spending more than three or four days above 7000m, because you will experience weight loss, worsening appetite, poor sleep, increasing apathy and minor ailments such as a viral sore throat or chest infection.

At extreme altitude, site the base camp at or below 5000m, so that proper recovery can take place between sorties to higher elevations.

EXPERT TIP

Dr Jim Duff
www.treksafe.com.au

'If someone is very ill at altitude and you can't figure out why, the patient should be rewarmed, rehydrated, resugared and reoxygenated (using descent, bottled or hyperbaric means).'

AMS is best prevented by sensible acclimatisation, but acetazolamide (DIAMOX) can be used in an attempt to make the process of acclimatisation more comfortable or to minimise the symptoms of AMS. It increases your rate of breathing, thereby improving oxygenation during sleep. Side effects include an increased need to pass water, tingling in the fingers and toes, and carbonated drinks taste flat. It has not been shown to have an effect above 7000m.

Half of one tablet (125mg) should be taken twice daily as a trial at home for two days, several weeks before a visit to altitude. Assuming no unpleasant side effects are experienced, take the drug in the same dose for three days before staying at 3500m and thereafter for two or three days until you feel acclimatised – for about five days in all.

Acetazolamide is a sulfonamide medication, and persons severely allergic to sulfa medicines should not take it.

WARNING

Sleeping pills can be dangerous and actually predispose you to altitude sickness, because they depress your respiration, reducing your oxygen uptake. Melatonin is a sleep aid that has no contraindications at altitude. Also buy a good mattress, stay warm and relax.

!

Retinal haemorrhages
If they interfere with vision, descend.

Snow blindness
Extremely painful and serious. Caused by UV light damaging the cornea. Wear eye protection, even if the sky is totally overcast, as the UV still penetrates and rebounds off the snow.

Sleeplessness
Huts at altitude are difficult places to sleep, but don't worry; if you can lie for 8 hours at rest with a relaxed mind and body it is the equivalent of 6 hours' sleep.

Weight loss
Altitude affects your digestive system, so you will experience weight loss. On a three- to six-week expedition to altitudes over 3600m (11,811ft), expect to lose 5–8kg (12–17lb).

Deydration
Lowered oxygen levels and AMS stimulate urine flow, so be sure to drink enough to keep your urine pale and plentiful.

Peripheral oedema (swelling of hands and feet)
Symptoms usually disappear after several days, and it is not an indication of HACE or HAPE.

THE ALPINE ENVIRONMENT

The weather in the European Alps is dominated by weather systems similar to those affecting the UK, with depressions and fronts coming from the Atlantic. The weather patterns in the Alps are also affected by the Azores High that pushes the Atlantic depressions northwards, resulting in longer stable periods of good weather. The Alps also make their own weather, which can be both extreme and unpredictable with violent thunderstorms, gusting winds, hailstorms and torrential downpours. (For more information on weather see *Rucksack Guide: Mountain Walking and Trekking*.)

Fig. 18 *The Alps make their own weather (a developing alpine thunderstorm).*

TEMPERATURES

Temperatures can vary on open glaciers between –10°C at night and +30°C during the afternoon. This heat can cause wet snow avalanches, snow bridges to collapse and frozen rock to be released, which create large stone falls. The air is so dry that the lapse rate is 1°C per 100m, but when it is raining it drops to 1°C per 200m (see *Mountain Walking and Trekking*, A&C Black, 2008 for more information on lapse rates).

AVALANCHES

Summer in the Alps is characterised by lower snowfall, and it is not unusual for it to snow as low as 2000m. This means that there is a lot of snow falling higher up and any fresh snowfall can avalanche if the conditions are correct. However, the warmer temperatures, greater speeds of metamorphism and settling of the snow pack mean that avalanches are less likely in summer.

In very hot weather, or if soaked by rain, the old snow can peel off in layers, meaning full-depth wet avalanches are not unheard of. The problem for summer alpinists is that they have fewer options where they can travel due to less snow coverage and more open crevasses and, because the snow is wet, the recovery of a live avalanche victim is rare. The best tactic is to be up and down your route before the Sun can warm the snow. Snow pits and shovel tests will not tell you more than you already know and are rarely performed in summer.

STONEFALL

Rock in the high mountains should always be treated with caution because it is subject to a constant freeze/thaw cycle. The orientation of the climb to the Sun affects the route, and on popular routes other people can present considerable objective dangers.

- Wear a helmet, but remember that the rest of your body is also vulnerable.
- Avoid gullies when it is warm or has just rained.
- Ask for local advice about the conditions on your route.
- Start early and climb quickly.
- Be careful when cleaning loose rock from routes.
- Rest where you are not exposed to rockfall.

THE ALPINE ENVIRONMENT

Intense heat in the Alps generates huge thunder-storms and lightning, which usually appear in late afternoon and form suddenly even during a spell of good weather. Warnings of imminent lightning are:

- Thunder, even without any visible lightning
- A sudden cloudburst of enormous raindrops or huge hailstones
- Signs of highly charged air such as hair standing on end
- Crackling noises or buzzing in the air
- Equipment humming
- Small sparks given off around metal objects
- A bluish glow around objects (St Elmo's Fire).

Direct lightning strikes are rare, and you are more likely to be hit by a side flash or ground current as it arcs to find an easy way to ground.

If you are caught in a thunderstorm:

- Get off the highest location (even a few metres lower may offer some protection).
- Stay away from taller trees and out of depressions, gullies or water.
- Avoid caves and overhangs unless they are dry and unless you have 6m of headroom and 2m of space on every side.
- If you are prevented from descending, remove metal objects, occupy as little area as possible and sit, crouch or stand on your pack with your hands and feet off the ground.

Fig. 19 *Caves and overhangs are dangerous places to shelter in a lightning storm. Minimise your contact with the ground, as ground currents can be very strong and can enter the victim in this way.*

Fig. 20 A cornice on the Monch, the Alps, which collapsed not long after this photo was taken, taking a climber with it (luckily, he survived).

An alpinist with great technical skills but poor route-finding technique is in more danger than if his skills were reversed. Alpine navigation is mostly done by map reading alone, as the geographical features are large and easily identified. A compass is rarely used, but it may be useful to orientate yourself for a descent or when it is dark or misty. Altimeters are useful to identify your location on the route and the distance to the summit.

MAP VARIATIONS

Alpine maps of mountainous areas use a 3D shading effect to indicate relief. The French Alps have a 10m vertical interval that changes to 20m when you cross into Switzerland, Germany and Austria, sometimes on the same map! The magnetic variation is small and is largely ignored. Beware that glaciers are largely retreating and changing shape annually and the snout may be further back; marked routes may be impassable, crevasses shown on the map may not be there and blank areas may have crevasses.

A GPS:

- Picks up signals from satellites.
- Calculates your position and displays it as a latitude and longitude fix to the nearest 1/100th of a minute or as a grid reference.
- Gives the direction, the speed at which you are moving, the distance to a location and the altitude.

The receiver needs to pick up signals from at least three satellites – more satellites provide greater accuracy. Like any other position measuring device, a GPS isn't perfect. Officially, positioning with 95 per cent confidence will be accurate to better than 20m, but in effect it will often be much better than that.

GPS AND MAPS

When relating the position given by a GPS to a map a problem arises. Different countries have their own datum in which their country is mapped – if your GPS is not set to the right one, it can place you as much as several hundred metres off route. There are dozens of selectable datum pre-loaded into a GPS so that it can be used anywhere in the world. In 1984, a world geodetic survey was published and it is now possible to produce maps and charts of the Earth's surface to a common datum – WGS84. Many countries are converting their maps to the WGS84 datum, but check first.

PROBLEMS WITH GPS

A GPS can provide very accurate information but, for mountain navigation, it is only an aid; traditional map and compass skills remain the backbone of sound navigation. Relying solely on a GPS would be foolish, considering:

- The batteries can run flat.
- There are still times when GPS can give a bad position without warning.
- Users of GPS in high northern latitudes will receive signals from satellites at relatively low elevations to the south of them. These may then be obscured by steep ground.
- A signal error may occur if the receiver is close to large reflective objects such as boulders or cliffs.
- Severe weather conditions can prevent you from operating your GPS – pressing small buttons while wearing gloves and reading the screen in a storm can be difficult.

NAVIGATION

ADVANTAGES OF GPS

A GPS is an aid in complex and featureless terrain, where traditional map-and-compass navigation is tricky e.g. crossing ice caps or a poorly mapped area.

A GPS can:

● Give a very accurate grid reference of your present location.

● Provide the facility to return to within a few metres of a previously visited location by marking a 'waypoint' at the location (useful in bad weather).

● Allow you to enter the grid reference of a specific point you want to go to.

● Show you the bearing and distance to the next objective, but when a GPS unit indicates you are 1 mile from a designated spot, that is an 'as the crow flies' mile, not a mountain mile.

● Track positions all day for later comparison with the map.

● Link with digital maps to upload waypoints or routes, email waypoints to friends and download your track to a map.

DON'T FORGET

When following a 'GO TO' direction on a GPS, it is very easy to ignore the ground under your feet, to leave the map in your pocket and to forget about the contours. You can get into a situation where you are lost, relying solely on only your GPS, and at the mercy of technology.

An altimeter measures atmospheric pressure just like a barometer and turns it into an estimation of altitude, using either a dial with a needle or a digital display. Since the weather is caused by high and low pressure systems, you must regularly calibrate the altimeter by setting it when you are at a known elevation. An altimeter can also be used for navigation:

- Knowing your exact altitude can help you to pinpoint your position, especially on large uniform slopes and ridges.
- Altimeters can be more useful than a map in poor visibility or places where a map is not of much use such as a rock climb.
- Altimeters are particularly useful when accurately following a contour line for any distance.
- They help you descend and ascend to a specific point (note the target altitude from the map, but 'aim high' when coming down from above and 'aim low' when coming up from below). You can even set your altimeter alarm.
- Combined with slope aspect an altimeter can position you more accurately.
- It can help with planning ahead e.g. how much height is left to reach a summit? Have you reached the summit? How far down is halfway?
- You can monitor your progress through the day – if it has taken one hour to climb the first 400m and you have another 700m to go, then you can expect it to take at least two more hours to get there.

ALTIMETER LIMITATIONS

The pressure graph
Air pressure does not decrease uniformly as you ascend, but altimeters approximate that it does over small ranges. Reset it to a new reference altitude after changes in height of several hundred metres.

Weather changes
Small changes in air pressure significantly change the altitude reading, so recalibrate every few hours.

Temperature effects
The altimeter uses a list of average air temperatures for different altitudes. The problem is that the air temperature in your location is unlikely to be exactly the world average for that particular altitude. Regularly set the altitude at known points to minimise any effects. In cold weather (below 15°C at sea level/freezing level of 2400m) an altimeter tends to under-read any altitude changes. Conversely, in hot weather it tends to over-read changes.

Wind effects
An increase in wind speed due to air flowing around an object creates a drop in pressure where the wind speed is highest. Conversely, if you set the altimeter out of the wind, and then use it somewhere much windier, it might read too high.

View from Gran Paradiso, Italy, looking towards Mont Blanc

WHEN AND WHERE TO GO

Global warming and the fickle nature of the weather means that it is best to be flexible with your goals until you have a sense of what alpinism is like. Some mountains have a small window of opportunity that opens and closes erratically during the season, e.g. the Matterhorn.

The summer season is from June to September, but for easier routes and valley rock climbing the season is longer. Winter conditions in the European Alps occur anytime between October to May, with the 'official' winter season running from 21 December to 20 March. Crowding is a problem in popular areas, especially in France during August. However, there are always quiet places for the truly adventurous mountaineer.

Today there is rarely enough snow in winter and spring to maintain the condition of the steeper snow and ice faces throughout the summer. Spring may be a better time for snow routes, but then you may require skis or snowshoes for approaches and the avalanche danger is real. Conversely, technical rock routes may be better when the snow has melted later in the season.

Fig. 21 L'eveque, Arolla, Switzerland

There are thousands of great mountain climbs in the European Alps. Some of the more popular areas are:

Switzerland

- **Arolla** The Swiss Valais is an ideal location for a first season, as it has a great variety of short and easily accessed mountain routes and some simple glacial treks and hut walks.

- **Bernese Oberland** Perfect for those interested in traditional, non-technical alpine mountaineering and a great place to trek from hut to hut.

- **Saas Fee and Saas Grund** The Saastal is not as popular as its close neighbour Zermatt, but offers some of the best non-glacial walking routes in the Alps and plenty of scope for multi-day mountaineering traverses. Close by are the wonderful peaks of the Mischabel chain and the plentiful 4000m (13,123ft) peaks around Zermatt.

- **Zermatt** The Matterhorn makes it a busy and expensive place, disfigured by extensive skiing apparatus. It is the valley base for a host of famous 4000m (13,123ft) peaks, but stay elsewhere and make a short trip to climb specific routes.

- **Grimsel/Furka Pass** A fantastic area for high quality, accessible rock climbing in an alpine setting and for mid-range, low altitude alpinism.

- **Bregaglia and Bernina** A spectacular range of granite peaks with good quality rock climbing. The Bernina has some snow and ice classics.

France

- **Chamonix** A superb choice of routes on rock, snow and ice, and with some imagination crowded routes can be avoided. There are more challenging climbs and, besides Mont Blanc, there are 13 other 4000m (13,123ft) mountains. The Tour du Mont Blanc is a justifiably famous trek.

- **The Ecrins Massif** A beautiful place offering a wide selection of climbs. There are few cable cars and the walks to peaks and huts are long. The peaks are generally lower, and because it is further south, it has more reliable weather, but snow disappears rapidly.

Italy

- **Dolomites** If you are after longer, steeper rock routes and Via Ferrata, then you cannot beat the Dolomites; the scenery is superb and the trekking is awesome.

Fig. 22 The Dent du Geant,
Chamonix, France

Alpine routes (even easy ones) are long, exposed and involve a lot of height gain and loss. However, some routes are possible to complete in a day through access via téléphériques and railways, but only if you can move swiftly.

There can be several types of climbing in the same route and the weather can change the grade overnight. Add to this big boots, a rucksack, long run outs, loose rock, crevasses, moving together, the altitude and the descent when you are tired, and it can all seem a tall order!

Build your experiences gradually and travel lightly, and the Alps are a much less daunting place.

Before going:

- Plan and prepare for all eventualities
- Practice specific skills such as crevasse rescue
- Choose and research your route
- Watch the weather.

MENTAL PREPARATION

Fear is natural; the mark of a good alpinist is how they cope with it. Your state of mind is as important as your technical skills in avoiding accidents. Three factors have been found to frequently contribute to accidents:

1 **Ignorance** You will never know everything, and you can learn something from everyone. Practice as much as possible, e.g. do not leave learning how to prusik until you are down a crevasse.

2 **Casualness** Most accidents occur on easy ground when your guard is down. Be vigilant, become self-sufficient and do not climb expecting to be rescued.

3 **Distraction** Anxiety, sore feet, pleasure at gaining the summit and forgetting that the climb is only half over, relying on a more experienced partner can all take your focus away from the climb. Keep your mind on the bigger picture.

PHYSICAL PREPARATION

Start your training several months in advance; climbing easy routes with big boots and a rucksack is the best training for alpine peaks. Improve your aerobic capacity and your strength, but remember that with good technique you use up less energy.

DON'T FORGET THE SKILLS

Familiarise yourself with summer mountaineering, scrambling and snow and ice skills before venturing to the Alps. Competence in these skills is essential for tackling the harder peaks.

Fig. 23 Study the map and guide book carefully before you head off – knowledge without understanding is dangerous.

DEVELOP GOOD JUDGEMENT

Safe mountaineering requires judgement, but remember: what worked well in a given place at a given time may not be appropriate in the same place at a different time. Judging any situation by protocol or rules invites disaster. Aldous Huxley said, 'Experience is not what happens to you. Experience is what you do with what happens to you'. Listen to the messages your body and the environment give you – the weather, temperature changes, speed of the team, your kit etc., and choose the appropriate course of action. Ultimately, safety and risk reduction is about being aware of danger – but remember: what is dangerous for one team may not be dangerous for another, so do not simply follow what others are doing.

KNOWLEDGE IS POWER

The Alps are in a constant state of change and much of your planning and preparation at home can save time on the mountains.

- Check your route description in local guidebooks and magazine articles and seek up-to-date information about your route from other climbers and local guide offices.

- Internet sites provide up-to-the-minute alpine climbing conditions with climbing forums. Professional Mountain Guides give good information, even if they do err on the side of caution.

- Guidebook times are averages for acclimatised, fit, competent parties who know where they are going and how to climb quickly.

Climbing in the Alps doesn't rely so much on what grade you can climb, but on what grade you can climb fast! Start with an easy climb, two technical grades inside your limits, so that you can assess how quickly you move. The harder and more committing the climb, the finer the line you will have to tread between safety and adventure, and the greater judgment and experience you will require.

Ask the following questions:

- How long is the approach and what type of approach is it?
- How long is the route, and are you fit enough to move fast?
- Does it stay safe all day?
- Is it in condition?
- How do you get down?
- Have you booked a hut or is a bivvy better?
- What is the weather forecast?
- What equipment do you need to take and what can you leave behind?

EXPERT TIP

Graeme Ettle
BMG/IFMGA Guide
www.Graemeettle.com

'Get to the climbs early to avoid teams above your head.'

Fig. 24 *Wisdom in the mountains is not about being absolutely correct, but correct enough.*

The grading of an alpine climb is fundamental to selecting a route. The most common grading system in the European Alps (except for the Bernese Alps and sometimes the Eastern Alps) is the International French Adjectival System (IFAS).The overall grade describes the difficulty of the route and is combined with the UIAA or French rock grading system to describe the rock pitches. The technical ice rating numbers are about the same as in the USA or Canada. The overall grade combines:

- Altitude and length
- Length and difficulty of approach and descent
- The number of difficult pitches and how sustained they are
- The exposure
- Adequacy of stances
- Popularity
- Difficulty of retreat
- Quality of the rock, snow, ice and in-situ gear
- Objective dangers
- The hardest section – at the top or the bottom
- Orientation of the route to the Sun
- Exposure to the weather.

The difficulty and seriousness of a route grade is also affected by the current conditions – crevasses open up, bergschrunds become impassable, and straight-forward ice/snow may be technically difficult mixed climbing. Rock can become verglassed or even snow covered, sometimes making life easier. The overall grades have a '+' or '–' to indicate minor differences.

See the table overleaf for further information on various grades.

ALPINE GRADING SYSTEM	
Grade	**Description**
F Facile (easy)	Straightforward, possibly a glacier approach and very simple scrambling. The snow or ice will be of an easy angle, e.g. Allalinhorn, West Ridge and Aiguille du Tour.
PD Peu Difficile (a little difficult)	Routes may be longer and at altitude with snow and ice slopes up to 45 degrees. The glaciers are more complex, the scrambling is harder and there are more objective dangers, e.g. Mont Blanc, Goûter Route (PD–), Jungfrau (PD+) SE Ridge and the Gran Paradiso (PD–).
AD Assez Difficile (fairly hard)	Snow and ice at 40–55 degrees. Rock climbing up to grade III, but not sustained, e.g. Matterhorn Hornli ridge (AD–); Aiguille du Chardonnet Forbes Arête (AD).

Fig. 25 Facile: Point du Vausson, Arolla, Switzerland

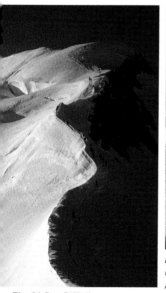

Fig. 27 Assez Difficile Aiguille du Chardonnet, the Forbes Arête is the LH skyline ridge and one of the best AD routes in the Alps.

Fig. 26 Peu Difficile: Mont Blanc, Chamonix

ALPINE GRADING SYSTEM	
Grade	**Description**
D Difficile (hard)	More serious with rock climbing at IV and V and snow and ice slopes at 50–70 degrees, e.g. Eiger Mittellegi Ridge, Aiguille du Chardonnet, North Buttress (D–) and the Aiguille du Midi Frendo Spur (D+).
TD Tres difficile (very hard)	Routes at this grade are a serious undertaking with high levels of objective danger. Sustained snow and ice slopes at 65–80 degrees. Rock climbing at grades V–VI, with possible aid, e.g. Mont Blanc du Tacul Gervasutti Pillar TD/TD+; the Matterhorn North Face.
ED Extremement difficile (extremely hard)	Exceptional objective danger, vertical ice slopes and rock climbing VI–VIII with possible aid pitches, e.g Eiger, North Face 1938 Route (ED2); Grandes Jorasses, Walker Spur (ED1).
ABO Abominablement difficile	Self-explanatory!

Fig. 28 Difficile: The North Face of the Tour Ronde, Chamonix

Fig. 29 Tres Difficile: Swiss route, Grand Capucin. Chamonix

Fig. 30 Extremement difficile: North Face, the Eiger (ED2), Bernese Oberland

Technical grades also inform you about a route's seriousness. If the technical difficulty is low compared to routes of a similar grade, the route is likely to be long and/or serious. The opposite is true of a route with high technical difficulties when compared to similarly graded routes; it is likely to be short, unserious or have a short, difficult crux section.

TECHNICAL DIFFICULTY OF THE ROCK
The UIAA scale (Roman numbers) or French sport grade is given. Generally, the longer the route, the less severe the rating, therefore, if a pitch is 6a in the valley, the same pitch on a mountain route would possibly be given 6b. Add to this no bolts, heavier clothing, footwear and a rucksack and the climbs will feel harder than an equivalent route in the valley.

TECHNICAL DIFFICULTIES ON SNOW AND ICE
Some guidebooks give the steepness of the snow/ice sections, but for longer routes only an average angle may be given and steeper sections missed out. On genuinely steep routes, the ice grading system is often used, most commonly the Water Ice grade, but sometimes the Scottish grade, is given (*see* Appendix, p.128).

TECHNICAL DIFFICULTY OF MIXED SECTIONS
The UIAA rock grading system is often used, even though it does not tell you much about the actual difficulty. Sometimes the WI-grade system is used (M-grade).

The advantage of many European alpine bases is their ski infrastructure, with cable cars to shorten the walk to the hut or the route. However, this can also destroy the feeling of remoteness and adventure.

Using a cable car

Téléphériques, cable cars and trains are often crowded, but there is no need to rush to be sure of a space. Good etiquette will prevent injuries.

- Remove your rucksack and put it on the floor with the waist belt wrapped around it to prevent buckles being broken.
- Carry your ice axe and ski poles in your hand.
- Keep your crampons inside the rucksack.

***Fig. 31** Walking routes in the Alps are marked on rocks and trees with white/red/white stripes. When the track ahead is difficult the marks become white/blue/white.*

Wild camping is officially frowned upon, and in some countries it is against the law. Bivvying, however, is acceptable in some countries from sunset to sunrise, although not in the vicinity of a hut.

There are two reasons to bivvy:

1 An emergency or unplanned night out
2 A planned bivvy, because the route is too long or you just want to enjoy a night on the mountain.

The problem with planned bivvies is that you need to ensure you carry enough equipment to allow for a reasonable nights' rest, whereas spending a night in an unplanned bivvy is often miserable.

BIVVY SITE
Your first task is to select a sheltered site. Keep in mind the mountain features, which are above you, but are not visible in the dark. Ridges may be exposed to wind, so be sure to move down the side of the ridge; and chimneys, although potentially large enough to accommodate you, can transform into a rock waterfall.

Fig. 32 *Bivvying on a route is something all climbers should experience at least once (Dave Williams, The Walker Spur, Chamonix, France).*

The difference between a good night and a bad night is down to the details. The following may help:

- Remain tied into your anchors and wear your harness inside your sleeping bag.
- To prevent water wicking along the rope, keep it lower than you, before it enters your sleeping bag, and tie a couple of knots between yourself and the anchors.
- You should have enough rope to reach the furthest points on your ledge, but it should be easily adjustable – a prusik from your harness to the attachment rope via a 60cm sling will allow you to stay tight on the rope wherever you are.
- A handrail between two anchors is useful for clipping gear.
- Take a warm bottle to bed to keep you warm and force moisture out of your bivvy bag.
- Remove damp socks and put them against your body, and keep a pee bottle near by.

Fig. 33 *If you need to use a plastic bivvy bag, pull it over your head and punch a few breathing holes into it.*

BREATHABLE BIVVY BAG

A breathable material is essential for long-term bivvies, but avoid heavier models with hooped poles. A bivvy bag with a cowl keeps spindrift and rain out and helps to seal you into the bag without having to zip yourself in completely. Try not to breathe directly into your bag, and if you are forced to seal yourself in, leave a gap to breathe through.

SNOW CAVES

Snow caves provide much more shelter than bivvy bags or small tents, but it is rarely possible to dig them in the Alps in summer.

SLEEPING MATS

Closed cell foam is bulky, but inflatable mats puncture. If you are planning a bivvy, cut your closed cell foam pad into three or four sections and rejoin them by sewing and taping, which allows you to lay the mat flat against the side of your rucksack. Alternatively, use the pad from your rucksack and stuff your jacket and overtrousers under your legs. Your fleece jacket can act as a pillow.

EATING

You will be warmer if you are well fed and watered, because digestion releases heat.

- Carry a small gas stove and use a small steel cup with a lid (instead of a pot) or a Jet Boil stove.
- For an ultra lightweight bivouac carry ready-to-eat food and use the stove only for melting water.
- Heating several small quantities of water is more fuel-efficient than one large quantity.

Bivvying without a sleeping bag is usually miserable! Instead of carrying a bivvy bag, you could try a Blizzard Bag, which is small, light and warmer, although condensation is a problem and the bag is difficult to pack small again.

- If you do not have a closed cell pad, sit on your climbing ropes or your rucksack.
- If you are stuck on a steep, small ledge, improvise a seat from your backpack or a padded rope to ensure blood can flow to your limbs.
- If you can abseil down to a ledge and jumar back up, do it.
- If you are carrying food, have a bite to eat and brew up a hot drink once in a while.
- You can still get into your sleeping bag, even on a standing bivvy, but stay tied to the anchors.

EXPERT TIP

Alun Richardson
IFMGA/BMG Guide
www.alunrichardson.co.uk

'If you do get caught out loosen the laces on your boots to keep the blood flowing. Also don't be afraid to continue even if it has gotten dark.'

Make sure you carry enough emergency gear to survive a night out (Aiguille du Plan, Chamonix, France).

Huts enable walkers and climbers to get an early start without carrying heavy bivvy gear and lots of food. National Alpine Clubs own most of the huts, but some are privately owned. They vary from small bivvy huts with no facilities, to large mountain hotels with showers and single rooms.

The average hut has dormitory beds and a guardian who provides a three course evening meal and breakfast. In popular huts the guardian usually purchases the franchise for the hut and makes their living from supplying the food and drink. In France you can bring and cook your own food in a separate area of the hut; in other countries it is forbidden or you must give your food to the guardian to cook for a small charge.

Huts are open from mid-June to mid-September and the most strategic stay open during the ski touring season, but even outside these times a winter annexe without a guardian is always open. Huts can be crowded and some, such as the Mont Blanc huts, are booked months in advance. Book early by phoning the hut, and tell them if you decide not to go – you may be charged, especially in Switzerland.

UPON ARRIVAL

- Leave your sac, boots, crampons (inside your sac if they are in a bag) and ice axes in the entrance room (sometimes they are left outside).
- Book in immediately and carry ID.
- Rucksacks can be taken to many dormitories.
- Boots are banned inside, but slippers are supplied.
- Many huts have small baskets to help you organise your gear.
- You can hang gear up to dry, but do not spread it out all over the hut.
- Gear is rarely stolen, but in the morning rush things are often picked up by mistake, so ensure yours has your name on it.

Fig. 34 Approaching the Vignetts hut, Arolla, Switzerland

AFTER CHECK-IN

Once checked in, the guardian will assign you a room and bunks. The hut will have a number of wake-up calls depending on the route you are climbing, and you are likely to be in a dorm with people arising at the same time. It is normal practice to mark your bunk with some clothing when you arrive.

- Being organised is important: keep out your headlamp, drink, earplugs, toothbrush and toiletries for the evening only.
- People will try to sleep at all times of the day, so be quiet in the dormitory – if you must talk, go outside.
- Do not pack or fiddle with gear in the dorm – do it outside.
- Use your headlamp if necessary, but avoid shining it into sleeper's eyes.

DINNER

- Dinner is usually served at about 18:30, but on particularly crowded days there may be multiple sittings.
- After dinner it is polite to clear the table and wipe it with a cloth kept near the kitchen.
- During the evening you may have to tell the guardian what drink you would like for breakfast.
- Cold water is only sold in bottles due to health concerns, but hot water is available and is cheaper.
- If you take tea bags etc., you can make your own drinks.

SETTLING THE BILL

Typically the bill is paid in the evening after dinner (some huts take debit/credit cards, but be sure to ask when you book). If you are staying multiple nights in one hut, you can usually pay the bill on the last night.

Fig. 35 *Alpine huts are often busy and the guardians work hard looking after you (inside the Vignettes hut, Arolla, Switzerland).*

GETTING UP IN THE MORNING AND DEPARTING

Departing in the morning is often a manic rush as you try to get ahead of other teams.

- After rising, check your sleeping area for anything left behind and neatly fold your blankets.
- The skill to departing quickly is to pack your rucksack the night before and have the items you will need for the morning at the top.
- On many routes you will be wearing your harnesses all day, so wear it from the start.
- Water bottles and Thermos flasks are often gathered the evening before and filled by the following morning for a small charge.

GETTING TO YOUR ROUTE

Most routes, especially snow and ice faces, look much steeper in the dark and when looking at them straight on. Spend the evening before looking at your route on a map. Find prominent features that you can identify en route, and take a photograph with a digital camera and review it later. Do the same for the descent. It is advisable to walk the start of the approach in daylight to avoid wandering aimlessly around in the dark.

Start the approach slowly and speed up later; a stop-and-go tactic uses energy inefficiently, leaving you sweating. Eat and drink on the move or when you stop, for example, to put crampons on.

THE ROPE

A UIAA half rope is enough for glacier travel, but beware – the thinner the rope the more stretch and the harder it is for the prusik knot to grip the rope.

EXPERT TIP

Lorenz Frutiger
IFMGA Guide
www.expeditiongreenland.com

'The story about the tortoise and hare often holds true; a party moving steadily the entire day will be faster than the party that "runs" between long breaks.'

Swirling clouds in the Bernese Oberland

There are about 160,000 glaciers in the Polar Regions and high mountains of the world, and 75 per cent of Earth's fresh water is locked up in glaciers – but they are disappearing fast.

A glacier is formed by the accumulation of snow at high altitude. Gradually, the force of nature converts the snow to ice and the glacier is pushed downhill on a layer of water. For the alpinist there are two types of glacier:

1 **Wet** Snow covered, resulting in hidden crevasses
2 **Dry** Bare ice

Travel on dry glaciers is usually straightforward, but crampons are sometimes required. The best advice for travel on wet glaciers is to rope up, know how to avoid falling into a crevasse, and to understand rescue techniques should the worst happen, as rescuing someone from a crevasse is difficult.

GLACIAL MORAINES

Glacial moraines appear after the glacier has retreated, usually as linear mounds of rock, gravel and boulders within a fine powdery material (till).

● Terminal moraines are at the end of the glacier.
● Lateral moraines are on the sides of the glacier.
● Medial moraines are in the middle of two merging glaciers.
● Eskers are long, snake-like ridges.
● Drumlins are distinctive streamlined hills in the lowlands.

Walking on moraines can be safe, but there is often substantial rock fall on lateral moraines.

Crevasses usually form when the ice comes under tension.

● **Over a drop** Crevasses appear perpendicular to the glacier's flow. On steep drops, the glacier breaks into a chaotic jumble with huge blocks of ice (seracs) that can tumble without warning.

● **On a bend** The faster-moving ice in the centre pulls away from the slower ice alongside, resulting in radial cracks.

● **As the valley base widens** The ice spreads out and vertical cracks may appear running parallel to the direction of the glacier's flow.

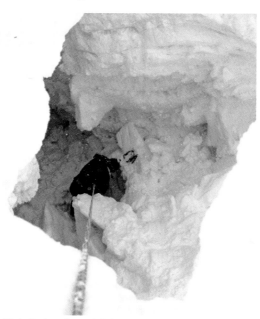

Fig. 36 *A climber after a fall through a snow bridge.*

There are a few indicators to help you identify crevasses hidden under snow. Look for dips in the snow as 'snow bridges' sag – especially after a long, warm period – and changes in surface colour after a snow-free period, when duller wind-blown snow tends to collect in the small dips. Conversely, after fresh snowfall without wind, brighter and lighter coloured fresh snow may collect in the dips.

CREVASSE RESCUE KIT

Carry the following kit when travelling on glaciers:

3 Prusik loops
Petzl Mini Traxion or Wild Country Ropeman
2 slings 220cm
1 revolver krab
2 long ice screws
1 abseil device
2 screwgate krabs

ROUTE FINDING

Alpine maps show likely crevassed areas, contour lines and even suggested routes to help you plot your route, but remember that glaciers change rapidly, especially with global warming. Take advantage of the times when you are high above a glacier to check your planned route, but do not assume that a trail or previously travelled route across a wet glacier is safe. The snow changes constantly and new crevasses can open up at any time to the point that what was safe in the morning may not be so in the afternoon.

Fig. 37 *Never travel un-roped on a wet glacier – you will be playing Russian roulette.*

WET GLACIERS – THE ESSENTIALS

- Cover your arms and legs and wear gloves.
- Crampons are essential unless there are many climbers on the rope.
- Everyone must carry rescue kit that is easily accessible, but ensure it is neat and does not hang below the leg loops on your harness.
- Keep an ice axe in your hand.
- If you are walking with ski poles, just use one.
- Use a rope and ensure there is a minimum of slack rope between you – do not carry hand coils.
- Don't gather together when stopping for a break; your combined weight may prove too much for a crevasse bridge.
- The most experienced member should lead to allow for the best route finding and pacing, but when descending on hard snow or ice, the most experienced and/or largest member should be at the rear.
- When crossing an obvious crevasse the rest of the team should move backwards.

When the route demands travel perpendicular to the crevasses (Fig. 38b) it may be appropriate to travel in echelon formation (Fig. 38a). This is safest when the location of crevasses is known. Echelon travel does have drawbacks, as it forces each climber to break their own trail, slows down the group, makes control of the rope more difficult and one climber may end up in a dead end.

Fig. 38 *(A) Echelon formation and (B) travelling perpendicular to crevasses*

WHEN TO USE A ROPE

A rope is essential when:

- you travel on wet glaciers in summer.
- you are travelling on unfamiliar wet glaciers in poor visibility.
- you are travelling downhill when the snow cover is shallow, low density, or variable (particularly early or late winter).
- visibility is poor.

Travel without a rope may be acceptable when:

- the glacier is free of snow, crevasses are clearly visible and visibility is good.
- you are skiing downhill when winter snow cover is deep, high density and consistent, and the terrain and crevasse patterns are known and/or easy to access.
- it compounds other problems, e.g. on avalanche terrain.

HOW MUCH ROPE IS REQUIRED?

The amount of rope between each climber depends on the terrain and the number of people on the rope. The important thing is to have enough rope available for a rescue plus a few extra metres to allow for rope stretch.

However, when there are large crevasses, when you are carrying heavy loads, or where you may have difficulty arresting a fall, you may need to increase the distance between climbers. This does, however, increase rope stretch, which can compromise communication, make it difficult to negotiate obstacles and may leave less rope for a rescue, but it is more important to stop someone falling into a crevasse in the first place. When there are long distances between climbers it may be prudent for the rear person to carry a separate section of 7mm rope for a rescue.

For two climbers using a 50m rope there should be eight to ten arm spans between the climbers; for three it is six arm spans. Take the remainder as chest coils (Fig. 42) or keep the excess rope in your rucksack (Fig. 43). For four or more climbers the distance is rarely more than four arm spans.

CALCULATING THE SPACING ON A ROPE
This system assumes that there are 30 arm spans in a 50m rope, but you must work out how many of your arm lengths it is and how many arm spans you have between people. If you are tying knots in the rope, you must allow more arm spans to enable the tying of knots.

A **Two people on the rope**. Spacing between the climbers is eight arm spans. Thirty arm spans, less two for tying in and eight between the climbers leaves twenty arm spans (ten coils on each person).

B **Three people on the rope**. Six arm spans between climbers (a total of twelve), three for the knots, leaves fifteen for chest coils on the first and last person.

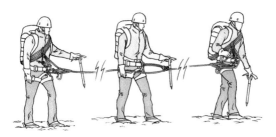

Fig. 39 Rope calculating system for travel across glaciers

USE OF KNOTS (Fig. 40)

To increase the chance of holding a substantially heavier climber, tie four or five large knots, 1m apart, close to each climber or just the heavier one (the first knot should be 1.5m away from the climber to allow the rope to bite into the snow). This is especially useful when the snow is hard, and/or on steep slopes where self-arrest is difficult. Using knots may complicate certain types of rescue, but the most important thing is to be able to stop someone falling in.

Fig. 40 *Tying four or five knots at each end of the rope can make it easier to hold a heavier climber, but can make rescue more difficult.*

Fig. 41 *Make sure you give enough rope when jumping a crevasse (Alpamayo, Peru).*

TWO CLIMBERS

With two climbers you have two options:

1 Tie in normally and take chest coils. This is particularly suitable when the terrain is changing constantly and the rope needs to be shortened and then lengthened (Figs 42 and 44) or you are carrying a heavy load where the coils act as a chest harness.

Fig. 42 Taking coils around the chest for glacial travel

2 Both mountaineers attach to the rope at just over one-third of its length using a figure of eight knot on a bight and back-to-back screwgate krabs or a re-threaded overhand knot. Carry the extra rope in the sac (Fig. 43).

Fig. 43 *One method of roping up for glacial travel (see also Fig. 44)*

MORE THAN TWO CLIMBERS
When there are more than two mountaineers, two attach using one of the methods above, the rest attach to the rope using:

- A figure of eight knot with two back-to-back screwgate krabs (to allow easy escape)
- A re-threaded overhand knot
- A lark's foot (Fig. 45).

Fig. 44 *Taking chest coils for glacier travel (note that there are two krabs on the prusik).*

USE A PRUSIK

In all situations attach a French prusik to the tie-in loop or karabiner on the harness via an opengate krab. Then attach an extra krab (an unscrewed screwgate) to the prusik to enable easy transfer of the load to an anchor (Fig. 43). If the terrain is serious, the middle person can attach two prusiks, one on each side.

Attaching a prusik ensures the load will come on to the pelvis and not the chest, which makes arresting a fall much easier. If you are the front person slide the French prusik towards the harness to create a chest harness.

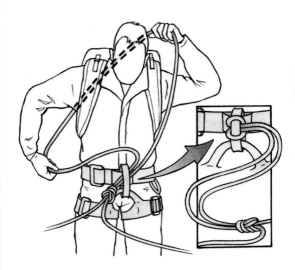

Fig. 45 *Using a lark's foot to attach to the middle of the rope. It creates a small attachment knot, but does make it difficult to get off the rope quickly.*

Crossing a glacier in
the Swiss Alps

The principles of crevasse rescue are as follows:

1 Arrest the fall
2 Create a rescue anchor
3 Transfer the load to the anchor
4 Assess the situation
5 Attend to the victim
6 Prepare the edge of the crevasse
7 Rescue the victim

PULLING OUT A SLED

In remote areas, the victim is often accompanied into the crevasse by a heavy sac and/or sled. It is unlikely that the victim and the pack and/or sled can be pulled out together, so the rescuers should consider hauling the packs or sled out first.

It is important to attach the sled from the rear to the safety rope by a prusik. This will prevent it from crashing on top of the victim. The hauler must also ensure that it is possible to detach from the sledge when down the crevasse.

USING ANCHORS AND BELAYS WHILE TRAVELLING

A fall into a crevasse generates small forces due to minimal acceleration and the friction of the rope cutting into the snow. This makes routine anchors and belays for crossing glaciers unnecessary, except on hard snow and steep slopes or when large suspect bridges have to be crossed. Any anchors placed must be strong enough to use for a subsequent rescue.

Fig. 46 *Crevasses can be cavernous – remain vigilant at all times to their dangers.*

Holding a fall into a crevasse is usually not difficult, but it can happen very quickly!

- When the climber falls, drop backwards and stamp your feet well in or hit the snow in the ice axe arrest position (Fig. 47).

- If you are minimising the slack in the rope, the chances are that the victim will have only fallen a very short distance into the crevasse and can get him-/herself out. If this is not the case, you will have to rescue them.

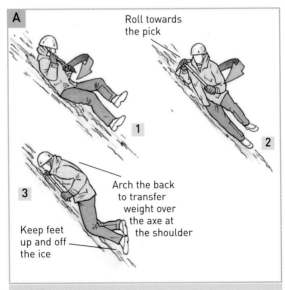

A

Roll towards the pick

1

2

3

Arch the back to transfer weight over the axe at the shoulder

Keep feet up and off the ice

Fig. 47 Ice axe arrest
A. On back
B. If pulled forwards
C. If pulled backwards

B

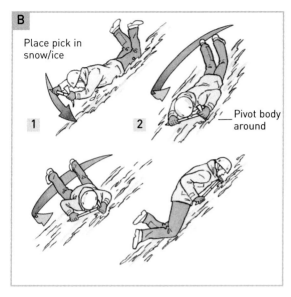

Place pick in snow/ice

1

2

Pivot body around

C

2

1

Pivot legs around

Place pick in snow/ice

Arch back

Lift feet

3

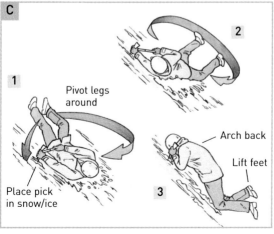

CREATING A RESCUE ANCHOR

Where the victim has fallen down the crevasse and cannot communicate, the rescuers must create an anchor strong enough to take the forces exerted by a pulley system:

● Crevasse rescue anchors are generally built at the location of the climber nearest the crevasse to reduce rope stretch.

● The closest climber can create the anchor, but in a team of three or more, this is best done by another climber moving forwards along the rope. They must slide their prusik along the rope to keep it taut to assist the climber holding the victim should they start to slide.

Transferring the load to the anchor

See Fig. 48 (opposite):

● Once an anchor has been created the loaded rope is transferred to it by rolling towards the sling attached to the anchor.

● The spare screwgate krab from the French prusik is then clipped into the anchor.

● Gently load the anchors by carefully moving towards the crevasse.

● When you are confident the anchor is holding, remove the opengate krab from your harness and back-up the prusik by immediately clipping the rope to the anchor with an HMS krab and a tied-off Italian hitch (Fig. 48).

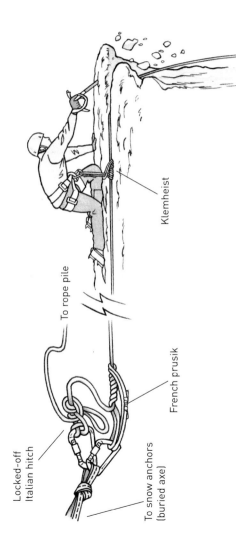

To climber

Klemheist

To rope pile

French prusik

Locked-off
Italian hitch

To snow anchors
(buried axe)

Fig. 48 *Transferring the load and approaching the edge of the crevasse*

CREVASSE RESCUE

The rescuer can now move to the edge of the crevasse, protected by a prusik or ascender (see Fig. 48, previous page), probing the snow to find the true edge of the crevasse. The edge of the crevasse will probably have to be prepared no matter what the next step (the exception may be if the victim's life is threatened, and speed is essential, or if the collapsing snow will injure them).

Remove overhanging snow to free the loaded rope, but take great care – a rope under tension is easily cut. Place a rucksack, ski pole or ice axe under the loaded or rescue rope at the edge and secure.

Once the edge is prepared you have a number of options in order of preference:

1 Lower the victim to somewhere they can climb out, or just to take the load from the rope.
2 It may be possible for the victim to climb out of the crevasse while being belayed from above.
3 Simply pull the victim out.
4 Perform a two-team pull.
5 Prusik out.
6 Hoist the victim (this is the last resort).

The worst-case scenario is a seriously injured victim – the rescuer should abseil to the victim using the other end of the rope. Pad the lip of the crevasse under the abseil rope and take a first-aid kit and warm clothing or a sleeping bag to treat and bundle the victim. The process of hauling out an unconscious victim can easily take over an hour (Fig. 49, opposite).

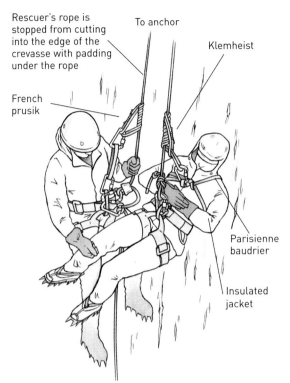

Rescuer's rope is stopped from cutting into the edge of the crevasse with padding under the rope

To anchor

Klemheist

French prusik

Parisienne baudrier

Insulated jacket

***Fig. 49** Descend to the victim and make them comfortable.*

- After treatment, make an improvised chest harness and clip it to a prusik on the victim's rope to keep them upright.
- To prevent the victim from suffocating by being dragged through the snow, turn them so that their back is against the wall of the crevasse.
- Retrieve any climbing gear the victim has with them, particularly prusiks, before ascending.

PRUSIKING OUT

An alternative to being pulled out by your friends is too prusik out:

- Remove your coils and undo them.
- Clip your rucksack into the loop of rope below you or attach it via a knot.
- Attach a foot prusik to the rope and ascend.
- It may be prudent for the rescuers to drop the other end of the rope for the victim to prusik up, rather than the line becoming jammed into the snow.

SIMPLE PULL

If there are enough rescuers, simply pull the victim from the crevasse (rescuers should not walk backwards unless they are sure that they will not fall into another crevasse). The rope to the victim should be belayed or protected via a prusik or ascender. If you feel resistance, do not pull any more; the victim may be at the lip of the crevasse.

TWO-TEAM PULL

If another team is available, the first team arrests the fall and holds the victim while the second approaches the edge and sends a rescue rope to the victim. If this team can do this quickly, it may not be necessary for the first team to build an anchor and transfer the load. If an anchor is not built, the first team belays the victim by moving backwards in the self-arrest position as the second team hauls the victim usually using an assisted hoist.

Top of the North face of the Tour Ronde, Chamonix

HOISTING USING PULLEYS

See Figs 50–2. Now things get serious; any pulley system will put an enormous load on to the anchors and, because of friction at the lip of the crevasse, all hoisting is strenuous and bad for your back. The rope will usually have cut deeply into the snow at the lip of the crevasse; whether this can be freed, how far the victim is into the crevasse, and whether the victim can help the rescuer will all dictate the method you use.

All hoisting methods have pros and cons, and follow the same principles as used in hoisting systems for rock climbing. **Note:** remember to release the Italian hitch and place the rope back through the karabiner before hoisting (Fig. 48).

EXPERT TIP

John Taylor
IFMGA Mountain Guide
www.montblancguides.com
'The middle man can place the waist belt of their rucksack underneath the rope to keep it away from their feet.'

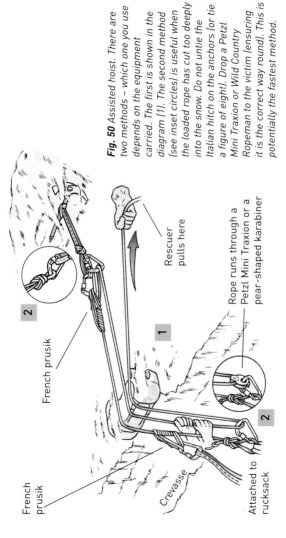

Fig. 50 Assisted hoist. There are two methods – which one you use depends on the equipment carried. The first is shown in the diagram (1). The second method (see inset circles) is useful when the loaded rope has cut too deeply into the snow. Do not untie the Italian hitch on the anchors (or tie a figure of eight). Drop a Petzl Mini Traxion or Wild Country Ropeman to the victim (ensuring it is the correct way round). This is potentially the fastest method.

French prusik

French prusik

Crevasse

Attached to rucksack

Rope runs through a Petzl Mini Traxion or a pear-shaped karabiner

Rescuer pulls here

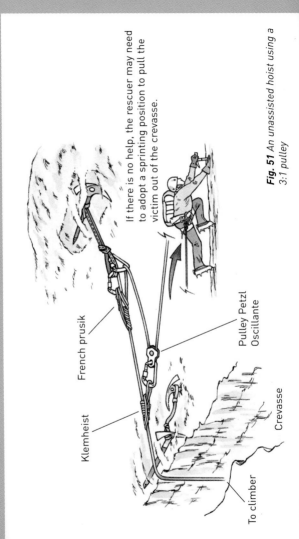

If there is no help, the rescuer may need to adopt a sprinting position to pull the victim out of the crevasse.

French prusik

Klemheist

Pulley Petzl Oscillante

Crevasse

To climber

Fig. 51 An unassisted hoist using a 3:1 pulley

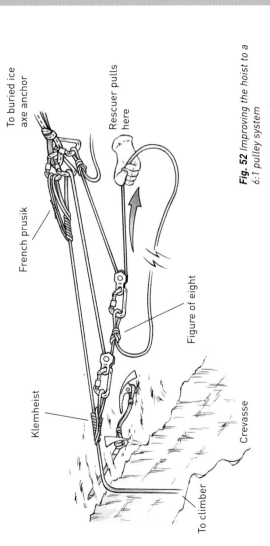

To buried ice axe anchor

Rescuer pulls here

French prusik

Figure of eight

Klemheist

Crevasse

To climber

Fig. 52 Improving the hoist to a 6:1 pulley system

The alpine climber must be versatile, efficient and capable of climbing quickly, placing protection rapidly and belaying while performing other tasks. The techniques are similar to those used for scrambling and winter mountaineering (see *Rucksack Guides* to *Rock Climbing* and *Winter Mountaineering*), but what makes alpine mountaineering a unique skill is that decisions must be made quickly and the skills used must be deployed much faster. Being fit, acclimatised and climbing lightweight will improve speed on all sorts of terrain.

Who you climb with is also important – a solid partnership in which you can trust each other to do the right thing at the right time and in which you can pick each other up when the other is down is something to be celebrated.

Climbers practiced in placing protection will find alpinism easier, because very few mountains routes are bolt protected. Alpine routes are rarely vertical, the run outs are long, the rock loose and wearing a rucksack increases the chance of falling upside down – taking a leader fall on an alpine route is not recommended.

ROUTE FINDING
- Preparation at home, on the approach and at the hut will simplify route finding.
- Do not blindly follow the marks of other climbers, although they may provide you with some clues: does the trail become fainter or do scratches disappear?
- Treat cairns with scepticism; they may be placed to help mountaineers retrace their steps, and not to show the way upwards.
- Fixed protection can be a good indicator that you are en route, but an abseil point may also show that you have gone the wrong way!
- Eventually you will develop a 'feel' for the right way as you absorb information subconsciously.

Fig. 53 *A solid partnership is essential for safe alpinism.*

ON SNOW

Moving together on steep slopes with a short rope between you can give an illusion of safety and a false sense of confidence. It is hard for rock climbers to accept that soloing in the Alps is a legitimate and often necessary practice ... but it is.

If you do decide to use short roping, beware that should one of you slip the other is likely to be pulled off, unless they are very quick and alert. It may be preferable and almost as quick to run the rope out and belay.

EXPERT TIP

Alun Richardson
IFMGA/BMG Mountain Guide
www.freedomphotographs.co.uk

'Don't copy what other climbers are doing unless you understand why – they may be making a mistake.'

ON EASIER ROCKY TERRAIN

Alpine routes have a lot of exposed, yet straight-forward, ground that is too risky to solo, but pitching it would take too long. Learning the skill of 'moving together' enables you to keep the risk acceptable and to move rapidly.

Your level of rock climbing expertise and your confidence will dictate the standard of ground on which you are prepared to move together, and the nature of the terrain will dictate the length of rope between each climber.

Fig. 54 *Moving together quickly and safely is the key to alpine success.*

ON DIFFICULT TERRAIN – SIMU-CLIMBING

This is a risky procedure, and both climbers must climb within their grade and understand the consequences of a fall.

Simu-climbing is when two (or occasionally more) climbers move together, at the same rate to reduce slack in the system, on ground that would normally be pitched. 'Bomb-proof' protection should be placed sparingly, but with consideration of the direction of the force a fall will exert on the equipment.

When the leader is down to a few pieces of protection, stop, set up a belay and, when the second arrives, exchange the gear.

Place a Ropeman or Tibloc on protection above crux sections to lessen the chances of the second pulling the leader off. This will hold the second should they fall, and prevent the leader being pulled off. This largely untested technique requires lots of practice to perfect and care should be taken to prevent rope damage.

It is particularly useful on snow or ice climbs, as there are no rope drag problems. For example, the leader places protection at the top of the difficulties, places a Ropeman on the protection and romps up the easy ground with the knowledge that the second cannot pull them off should they fall.

- Improve your personal climbing standard on rock and ice, and climb within your technical limits, enabling you to cruise through the harder sections. The second should follow rock pitches in half the time of the leader and ice pitches in a quarter of the time.
- Be fit enough for the climb you are tackling.
- Practice climbing wearing big boots and a sac.
- Practice climbing on rock with crampons.
- Practice your rope work until it becomes second nature and keep it neat and slick.
- Use direct belays whenever possible.
- Do not waste belay time. On pitched ground eat, drink and look at the guidebook while belaying.
- Using a Petzl Reverso on a direct belay means you can belay a second, but safely take your hands off the rope.
- Make changeovers at belays speedy and efficient. Three minutes saved on every belay on ascent and descent will save an hour over ten pitches.
- Eat and drink frequently to keep your energy levels up.
- When you stop to put gear on, work together – one flake the rope out, the other sort the rack.
- Organise your pack so that the gear you need first is on top.
- Swap gear quickly – bandoliers may be useful.
- Carry plenty of long extenders to reduce rope drag.
- On granite rock climbs with many smooth cracks cams are faster to place and remove.
- Look for fixed runners and belays, which can be used quickly, but check in situ gear and tat before using it.

- Place enough gear to keep you safe, but as little as possible.
- Climb without your rucksack on a difficult pitch, pulling it up afterwards.
- Pull on gear – ethics are great unless they kill you!
- If the route is at your limits, carry three rung etriers – do not rely on making them from slings and understand aid climbing.
- Maximise the strengths of the team. Plan ahead and ensure you and your partner lead on the ground you like best.
- On routes that are climbed in pitches lead in 'blocks'. Breaking the climb down into blocks means:
  - The leader can get mentally 'into the zone' for their four or five pitches.
  - The second can chill out and rest, rather than move straight into leading.
  - The leader can study the next pitch while belaying, which can help to speed up route finding.
  - You both stay warmer because no one person is sat on a belay ledge for too long.
- If leading in blocks, stack the ropes so that the leader's ends come from the top of the pile. You can start to re-stack the ropes once your second is just below you with the help of a Petzl Reverso on a direct belay.
- Climb light. Use twin ropes or a full-weight rope on very technical routes and carry a 5.5mm Dyneema line for pulling on abseils. This is a specialist technique, but has advantages when you have to haul, aid climb or jumar.

The summit is only halfway and the descent is invariably the most trying part of an alpine climb. Tired minds and bodies now have to cope with the most serious aspects of an alpine route – down climbing, loose rock and abseiling.

Route finding is difficult from above and this is when the work you did the day before to spy out the line of descent will pay off (p.78). Alternatively, bring a photo of the route.

DOWN CLIMBING

The method you use to descend will depend on the size and experience of the climbers plus the steepness and conditions of the descent. You may choose to down climb using the natural features to protect you. This technique is called short roping. You may decide to do a reversal of simu climbing where the lower climber places protection to protect the upper climber.

If you are short roping with the strongest climber above then the upper climber dictates the line to take, as they must decide whether they can hold a slip, need to lower you down or need to abseil. Tell the lower climber to stop as often as necessary for the upper climber to maintain a secure footing.

The important point to remember when everyone is moving together is that you maintain rope tension. Whatever you do, do not relax, stay vigilant and celebrate your success when you are back in the valley.

Fig. 55 *Descents from alpine peaks often involve down-climbing intricate ground with the rope on to enhance safety.*

At some point an abseil may be required. If you are not absolutely sure it is the correct way down, it may be quicker to lower your partner to check the route. If the route is incorrect, then it is easier to belay your partner back up.

There are often in situ abseil anchors on descents from classic routes. Always check the condition of both the tape and the anchors and, if you are in any doubt, back the system up with a good nut.

Repeated abseils down a long climb require you to be organised and have a method for rapidly attaching yourself and your partner to each belay.

- Tie a lark's foot sling to the abseil loop on your harness and tie a few knots to create loops for attachment at different points along its length ('cow's tail'). Then attach your abseil device to the first loop on the cow's tail or into your harness abseil loop.

- Do not throw the whole rope down. Instead:
  - Throw the rope down by layering the rope, doubled, across your hands (lap coiling) with decreasing sized layers.
  - Grasp the middle and throw this down, then do the same with the end of the rope.

- The first person abseils protected by a prusik.

- At the next belay, attach to it via the cow's tail, remove the belay device from the rope and tie the ends into the belay to possibly prevent a catastrophe should the upper abseil belay fail.

- Protect the second by holding on to the ropes.

- When the second has arrived pull the ropes down, feeding the one being pulled through the belay, ready for the next abseil.

- To identify the rope to pull, tie a figure of eight in the rope to be pulled, and an overhand in the other.

- When it is windy, take the rope down loosely fed into a rucksack.

COMMUNICATING

- Keep communications simple.
- Some teams use a loud whistle to mean 'rope free, come on down', as it's easy to distinguish from other teams who may be on the mountain, and can be heard in nasty weather.
- Two-way radios can be useful.

RETRIEVING AN ABSEIL ROPE

- Check before the last person abseils that the ropes will come down and that they are not going to become jammed in a crack.
- Extend the abseil station to move the rope.
- Separate and untangle the ropes before pulling. Remove knots and ensure you are pulling the correct one!
- Do not stand directly underneath the abseil.
- Pull ropes running through a sling slowly, otherwise 'glazing' damage can occur to the rope.
- If the rope remains stuck, try pulling at a different angle or pull heavily on both and then release the one you **do not** want to pull; the recoil of the un-weighted rope may free it.
- Finally get more people to pull. If the rope remains stuck and both ends are at the bottom, ascend on both ropes. If one end has disappeared part way up the rock, solo back to the anchors.
- Work together – while one member is pulling the ropes the other can be threading through the next anchor; as soon as the knot arrives, the first man down can attach the abseil plate etc., while the remainder of the rope is pulled down. This continuity is key to speedy abseiling.

Fig. 56 Getting to the top is only half of the journey!

Highly professional rescue teams that may work alongside voluntary rescue teams serve all alpine areas. Mountain huts usually have radios or a telephone; these and personal mobile phones are the most common methods of alerting rescue services. The usual international signals of six whistle blasts or six light flashes may be used, but should not be relied upon.

Mountain police, gendarmes and fire officers provide the French rescue service for free, but Swiss, Italian and Austrian mountain rescue is private and reimbursed by insurance fees. Insurance is a necessary evil, but it can lead to a false sense of security, evident in the increasing number and severity of accidents and rescues in the Alps.

Search and rescue experts are almost uniformly opposed to charging for their services, even in cases of negligence and stupidity, as it actually encourages more risky behaviour. They believe charging could delay requests for help, leading to worsening injuries, weather or other conditions, and ultimately to more difficult, dangerous rescues.

EMERGENCY NUMBERS

Emergency services telephone numbers are usually on maps and guidebooks, but should be checked at the tourist office or guides office.

UK	999
Norway/Sweden	112
Italy	113
Switzerland/France	117
(Wallis)	144
Austria	133
USA/Canada	911
Japan	110
New Zealand	111

Fig. 57 *Ensure that you have the emergency numbers pre-loaded into your phone (Peigne D'Arolla, French Alps).*

Helicopters can rescue stricken climbers quickly, but should not be relied upon, because they may not be able to fly or may be on another rescue mission. They pick up a casualty by landing or hovering just off the ground while the patient is taken on board or placed in a basket or stretcher. They can also hover and winch the casualty on board.

If you are waiting for a rescue:

- The wind created by a helicopter can reach 100kph. Clear the landing zone and surrounding area of all loose objects including vegetation, clothing and sacs. If you cannot do this, then tie them down.

- Helicopters cannot land on slopes of too much angle. A flat area of about 5m square is ideal, but there must be enough clearance for the helicopter's blades and tail in a 180 degree arc (hollows are not a good idea!) A helicopter tilts forward on take-off, so high ground that slopes away under the tail is best.

- If the helicopter is light enough to descend vertically or horizontally, it only requires enough room to hover. If it is heavy, a clear flight path is required.

- Mark your location with bright objects (the flash on your camera can be used to great effect).

- If the terrain is steep the helicopter will have to hover with the skids touching the ground, and there is a danger of the rotors hitting the slope if the terrain is very steep. It is likely it will drop off a rescuer and then depart until told to return. Hovering is risky when close to the ground.

- Helicopters perform better if they can take off and land into the wind. Indicate the wind direction using streamers or stand with your back to the wind, arms pointing in the direction in which the wind is blowing.

- Stay clear of the landing zone.
- If visibility is poor, a reference, such as a person or pack, on the pilot's side of the helicopter can be useful. Disturb the snow to allow the pilot to see the snow.
- Do not try to touch the helicopter or cable before it has made contact with the ground. Static charges build up in a helicopter when it is flying, which are discharged when the helicopter or a cable touches the ground (they can jump a metre).
- Helicopters are very noisy – protect your eyes and ears.
- Stay away from the helicopter and only approach it from the front when signalled to do so in single file.
- Drag rather than carry equipment such as skis.

Fig. 58 *Helicopters can rescue stricken climbers quickly, but they should not be relied upon.*

THE ALPS IN WINTER

The Alps in winter are an entirely different experience to summer. Temperatures fall to −25°C (−13°F), and you need to carry a heavy rucksack and wear big boots and thick clothing, all of which increases the weight you are carrying. You must learn how to move around efficiently and quickly, often on skis or snowshoes. The weather can change suddenly and you must be able to recognise avalanche terrain.

Alpine winters are not the place for first time alpinists and self-reliance is paramount. Your gear should be similar to that used for standard winter climbing, but with some additions:

● A powerful head torch and extra batteries, because you will be operating in the dark for longer periods.

● A balaclava or face mask.

● Plastic boots (essential).

● Spare socks and foot powder to dry your feet.

● Avoid sleeping in wet socks or inners, unless sitting in a bivvy with yiur feet in contact with the snow. Use an old sock to dry the inners.

● Mitts and a duvet jacket (essential).

See *Rucksack Guide: Mountaineering in Remote Areas of the World* for further information on mountaineering in colder climates.

During winter the Alps are riddled with frozen waterfalls. In good years, the season runs from November to April, with the most reliable conditions found in January/February. In March, the longer, sunny days can quickly ruin icefalls, but if you aim high then routes can still be found in condition.

Streams and melting snow create many of the ice climbs, but this means that there are often large snow bowls above the climbs that can create dangerous avalanche conditions after bad weather. North-facing bowls keep their avalanche conditions for a long time, so seek local information and look at the weather history. Scottish ice is predominantly snow ice, while alpine waterfall ice is often harder and more brittle. Temperature plays a big part in this however, and warmer days can result in perfect, soft, first-time placements.

European water ice grades range from 1–7 and are offset from Scottish grades by roughly one grade: a 4 in the Alps equates to Scottish grade 5 and French 5 is a Scottish 6. Several areas have gained worldwide acclaim due to a combination of quality climbing and ease of access. Below are a few ideas for climbing in Europe:

FRANCE

- **Ceillac** High up, so the conditions are usually good, plus there is only a short walk in.
- **Chamonix** A wide variety of grades, with the most popular at Servoz, Les Houches, the Mont Blanc tunnel entrance, Le Chapeau, Col des Montets, Le Châtelard and Argentière.
- **Fournel** Most routes are grade 4 or above, but there are some easier climbs. During snow, access is difficult and avalanche danger becomes a reality.

- **La Grave and the Argentière la Bessée on the fringes of the Ecrins National Park** Some are among the longest ice falls in Europe, but the south-facing routes quickly lose condition.
- **L'Alpe d'Huez** A ski resort great for novice/ intermediate climbers.

ITALY
- **Argentera Valley** Good for beginners and intermediate ice climbers, but the approach is long unless the road is still open.
- **Bardonecchia** The climbs are low altitude, therefore the season is pretty short (December to February).
- **Cogne** A wide variety of grades an hour's walk from the car. Situated on the Aosta Valley side of the Gran Paradiso National Park, it has a huge variety of over a hundred waterfalls.
- **Gressonay** A wide variety of accessible routes, but can be crowded.
- **Valle Varaita** Convenient, easy access and many routes.

SWITZERLAND
- **Kandersteg** The ice climbing mecca of Switzerland. Easy access and a wide variety of grades.

Be wary of old guidebooks, old timers and unrepeated routes – the grading system was completely overhauled in the early 1990s.

TECHNICAL GRADE

This refers to the technical difficulties of the pitch and takes into account the angle of the icefall, whether the climbing is sustained or not, the nature of the fall's formation, and the nature of its protection.

GRADE	DESCRIPTION
1	Easy angled ice that has no particularly hard sections
2	Easily protected pitch on good ice
3	Some 80 degree sections, but on thick, compact ice, with comfortable, well-protected belays
4	Sustained and near-vertical pitch, or a short pitch with a short, vertical section. Good ice and satisfactory gear.
5	Sustained and nearly always vertical pitch up discreet ice, or a less sustained pitch that is technically more demanding. Few rests.
6	Very sustained pitch that offers no rests at all. Difficult ice; some overlaps and other formations requiring good technique. Protection is difficult to place and often of dubious nature.
7	Very sustained pitch that offers no rests at all. Is extremely fragile and technically difficult ice. Protection is run-out or non-existent.

WATER ICE AND ALPINE ICE GRADES

Ice climbing ratings are highly variable by region and are still evolving. The WI acronym implies seasonal ice; AI is often substituted for year-round alpine ice and may be easier than a WI grade with the same number.

GRADE	DESCRIPTIONS
WI 1	Low angle ice; ice axe required. General angle: 50 degrees.
WI 2	Consistent 60-degree ice with possible bulges; good protection and anchors.
WI 3	Sustained 70 degrees with possible long bulges of 80–90 degrees; reasonable rests and good stances for placing screws. Generally good protection, and screws can be placed from comfortable stances. The ice is usually of good quality.
WI 4	Sustained climbing with some vertical sections, separated by good belays. The ice may have some technical features like chandeliers, but generally the quality of ice is good and offers secure protection and belays. General angle: 80 degrees.
WI 5	A long, steep, strenuous, columnar pitch of ice. Sustained with little opportunity to rest. Expertise in dealing with the different ice formations is required (e.g. chandeliers, cauliflowers, candled sections). Adequate protection, but requires effort to place. The climb may sometimes be run-out above protection. Belays may be difficult to create or hang. General angle: 90 degrees.

GRADE	DESCRIPTIONS
WI 6	A serious lead on severe or thin ice. Long vertical or overhanging sections, which leads to extremely sustained difficulties. There are few, if any, resting sites. Ice may not be of the best quality; often thin, chandeliered and hard to protect. Hanging belays of dubious quality may be required. General angle: 90+ degrees.
WI 7	Ice is very thin, long, overhanging or very technical. There are free-hanging columns of dubious adhesion. Protection may be non-existent. The pitch is very physical and emotional. Belays require a very high level of expertise, and may be marginal. This grade applies to only a handful of routes led by an even fewer number of world-class climbers. General angle: 90++ degrees.

MOUNTAIN WALKING AND TREKKING

This book is ideal for novices and experienced walkers alike, as it includes everything you need to know about how to navigate in the mountains. It includes information on weather, and tells you how to prepare for your trek, including packing your rucksack and the equipment you will require. It also demystifies the art of scrambling and tells you how to ascend Via Ferrata safely.

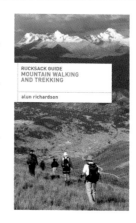

ROCK CLIMBING

Rock climbing can be a tough, sometimes dangerous, physical and mental challenge. This book covers everything you need to know to be safe when ascending steep rock formations, including efficient movement skills.

MOUNTAINEERING IN REMOTE AREAS OF THE WORLD

This is the essential handbook for planning and undertaking mountaineering expeditions around the world. It offers concise guidance, including where to go and when, advice on dangerous animals and minimising your impact on the environment, and dealing with extreme situations.

SKI MOUNTAINEERING AND SNOWSHOEING

Mountaineering on skis or snowshoes requires the ability to ski off-piste, good navigation skills, and awareness of the risks of the mountain environment in winter – you will find all of the above and more covered in this handbook.

WINTER MOUNTAINEERING

Mountains transformed by snow and ice are a world apart from lush summer slopes. This volume provides you with the techniques to explore wintry plateaus, tackle rocky ridges and ascend snowy slopes.